HAWK RISING

Maria Gianferrari

Pictures by Brian Floca

ROARING BROOK PRESS

New York

For Niko. For everything.
And in memory of Ezra.
—M.G.

For Sara, Jeff, Miriam, and
Hazel.
—B.F.

Text copyright © 2018 by Maria Gianferrari
Illustrations copyright © 2018 by Brian Floca
Published by Roaring Brook Press
Roaring Brook Press is a division of Holtzbrinck Publishing Holdings Limited Partnership
175 Fifth Avenue, New York, NY 10010
mackids.com

Library of Congress Control Number: 2017957293

ISBN: 978-1-62672-096-1

Our books may be purchased in bulk for promotional, educational, or business use.
Please contact your local bookseller or the Macmillan Corporate and Premium Sales
Department at (800) 221-7945 ext. 5442 or by e-mail at MacmillanSpecialMarkets@macmillan.com.

First edition, 2018
Book design by Monique Sterling
Color separations by Bright Arts (H.K.) Ltd.
Printed in China by RR Donnelley Asia Printing Solutions Ltd., Dongguan City, Guangdong Province

10 9 8 7 6 5 4 3 2 1

Father Hawk stretches wide his wings.

You stretch your arms
as Mars rises red
in the sky.

High in a backyard cedar they sit.
High from the window you watch.

Chicks jostle,
screech.
Beaks open wide,
waiting for breakfast.

Mother Hawk stays;
Father Hawk perch-hunts from a pole, silhouetted,
as sunbeams scratch the sky.
Red streaks spread.
Black talons curving onto wood.
Hooked beak, sharp as a knife.
Head turning.
Eyes searching.
Chicks waiting.

You noticing.

Sunbathing warms Father Hawk's outstretched wings,
drying drops of dew.
From the pole,
his sharp eyes spy a chipmunk.

He dives,
feet first,
wings arced:

fast
to
the
grass.

But Chipmunk scuttles under the neighbor's porch.

Father Hawk shakes his wings
and springs into the sky.

Keee-EEER,
Keee-EEER,

he calls,
circling,
seeking prey.

He rides the wind
like a wave,
twisting and turning,
kiting and floating.

Chicks waiting.
You watching.

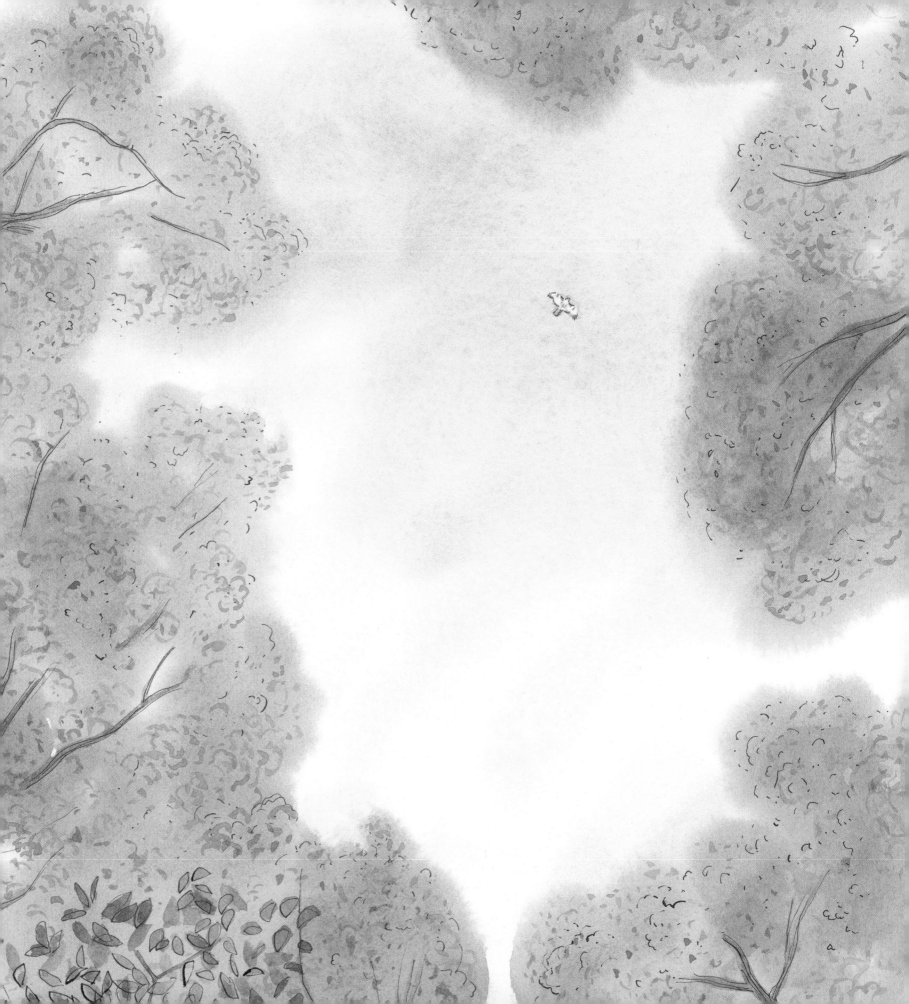

CAW-CAW-CAW

Crows charge
and chase,
darting and
diving,
driving Father Hawk from their roost.

He sails on the current
far from the crows
and alights on a limb
to perch-hunt
again.

Father Hawk's eyes sweep the lawn.
Back and forth they scan
greening grass for prey.
Sparrows sit and flit in bushes.

He leans—

then dives.

Crashing,
talons thrashing
in branches.

Once.
Twice.
Then again
and again.
Shielded by bramble,
Sparrows are safe.

Father Hawk takes to the sky,
riding and
gliding.

Shadows casting.
Chicks waiting.
You wondering.

Father Hawk lands on a light-pole.
Dandelions ripple.
Oaks tremble.

Father Hawk perches
and searches.
Sun sinking.
Daylight blinking.
Chicks waiting.

You fading.

Father Hawk spots
a squirrel scurrying
toward a tree.

He parachutes.
Legs tipping,
talons gripping . . .

and grabbing.

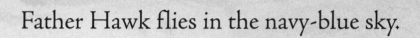

Father Hawk flies in the navy-blue sky.

Back in the nest
he lands.
Chicks screech
and jostle,
beaks wide open,
no longer waiting.

You yawning.

Through the night,
safe in your nests,
you and the Hawk family sleep . . .

until Mars rises red
in the sky
again.